Parenting Baby:
Solutions to New Parents' Dilemmas

Emily Jeffers

Contents

Introduction

Expecting a baby is a miraculous yet chaotic time. You hope to live the fairytale with a chubby, smiling, curly-haired baby out of a diaper commercial. You dream about its beautiful eyes, and how you and your partner will become even closer when that little bundle of joy arrives.

But as time ticks by and the due date nears, worries begin to arise. A million thoughts swirl in your head: How will I do this? Can I be a good parent? What if this happens, what if that occurs? You name it.

Some questions will dissipate as soon as you hold your baby in your arms. But others will persist and force you to find answers and prepare for the most important role of your life. That first year as a new family can be heaven on earth, or a complete disaster. What makes the crucial difference is your level of readiness. Emily Jeffers' book will help prepare you for parenting and enable you to be confident, relaxed parents who know what they're doing.

Here are answers to many of doubts and questions every new parent has, from the newborn's first day to its first birthday.

Your Newborn is Here!

Let's begin at the very beginning: meeting your baby for the first time. Yes, she is the light of your life, but...

"My newborn looks like an alien. Will this last forever?" you might ask.

When you hear the word "baby," you immediately think of the sweet, chubby-cheeked, silky-haired, cute faces from diaper commercials. Yet the wreck that was handed over to you in the maternity ward does not look like that at all.

On the contrary, your newborn with its large head, its frowning face and huge eyes, short legs and wide torso, reminds you irresistibly of E.T., Spielberg's sympathetic alien. But it's all normal, don't worry. In a few weeks, your baby will look like it's from this planet.

My baby seems to have a big head — is this normal?

Relax, dear. The head of a typical newborn makes up one-fourth of the overall length of the body. Some babies are born with an elongated head because of being in the birth canal too long. If the passage is tight, the head may be somewhat distended so it may look like the baby has a cone head (some mothers are given a birth infusion in order to avoid this). The baby may also have bruises or cephalohematomas that are the result of severe childbirth. All of these changes disappear after a couple of days and do not have any lasting consequences.

Is it normal for a newborn to have red spots on its body?

The skin of the newborn is thin and has a bluish color due to the blood vessels that are right below the surface. When the baby is warm, blood vessels spread and are easy to see as red spots because the skin is thin.

Immediately after being born, my baby looked like she was covered with cream. What is it?

Vernix caseosa protects the baby's skin while in the womb, swimming in amniotic fluid. If your baby had this substance on its body, it means she arrived on time. When the baby is born after the due date, the body almost does not have this overcoat, and the skin may be too dry.

Why does my baby have swollen eyes?

Swollen eyes are partly the result of a rather unpleasant time when coming into the world. Another reason, advocated by some scientists, is that the swelling serves as a kind of eye shield. Babies' eyes go from the darkness of the womb to being exposed to harsh light for the first time (usually strong hospital light).

If you are afraid that your baby will not see you because of the swelling, don't worry. Her eyes are not yet ready for sight at this point anyway.

What Is a Fontanelle?

The baby's skull was not formed in the prenatal period like the rest of the skeleton so that it would be able to pass through the narrow birth canal during labor. You will notice the fontanelle on your baby's head as a soft spot that pulses. It is actually a solid membrane that is located at the opening of the skull. The bones of the baby's skull will not grow immediately after birth in order to allow the baby's brain to expand, as it increases significantly during the first year.

How many fontanelles are there?

There are two fontanelles. The larger or front fontanelle is located at the top of the head, in the form of a diamond and can be up to two inches (five cm) wide. This fontanelle will close when the baby is one year (sometimes even a year and a half) old, and the closure process begins in the baby's sixth month.

The other fontanelle is triangular, less than one inch (1.5 cm) in diameter and is not easy to find. Usually, it is completely closed by the third month.

I notice that the fontanelle is pulsating. Should I be worried?

The fontanelle is normal if it's flat. If your baby has bright hair, you will surely notice a pulsation. This is completely normal. Also, when the baby cries, the fontanelle may pop out. This shouldn't worry you either.

If you notice your baby's fontanelle is a little tight, it could be a sign of dehydration. Breastfeed your baby or give it water to make sure it rehydrates, but in any case, contact your doctor immediately. The fontanelle, which is constantly protruding, may indicate increased pressure in the head and urgent medical attention is required.

You do not need to take special care of the parts of the head where the fontanelles are. It is only important that the baby's head is covered with a hat every time it goes out, until its first birthday. Regardless of the weather, but especially when it's cold or when the sun is shining, there should be some cloth or woolen protection over the fontanelles.

I'm a little afraid that I could injure the fontanelles while taking care of my baby.

There is no need for concern because you won't hurt your baby during ordinary care. Even older siblings cannot damage that solid membrane while playing with the new member of the family. Do not allow your unjustified fear to affect baby care because it can make you needlessly nervous.

Burping

Why should my baby burp after every feeding?

Burping is an important part of baby feeding. As the baby swallows milk, air inflates the stomach considerably, which can create an unpleasant sensation. She must be burping after feeding so this air doesn't bother her. After and during each feeding, the unnecessary accumulated air must be pushed out.

Bottle-fed babies should burp after about two ounces (fifty grams) of milk or after five minutes, while breastfed babies should burp after each breast.

Which position is the best for burping?

There are three ways the baby can be burped, and it's up to you and your baby to choose the best.

On the shoulder

Bouncing the baby on your shoulder gives the best results in most babies. The baby should be held against your shoulder. You can hold it under its bottom with one hand while gently patting its back with the other. Put a cotton cloth on your shoulder to protect your clothes.

Holding it in a sitting position

When doing this, support the baby's neck with your fingers while holding it upright with your thumbs under the armpits. Gently rotate the baby in a circular motion with its head tilted a bit forward in order to dislodge unwanted air. You may also pat or rub its back, taking care that the head does not fall back.

Face down

Turn the baby face down over your lap so that the stomach is against your legs.

Colic

Why do babies have colic?

The true cause of colic in babies is unknown, but there are several unproven theories about the causes:

- The baby has an intolerance to milk (yet breastfed babies have colic as well as babies on artificial formula).
- The intestinal tract is insufficiently developed and so spasms occur (spasms of the intestine).
- A temporary hormonal imbalance is present.
- The baby sucks too much air in with the milk, causing bloating.
- The newborn has a feverish temperament, often cries and is upset.
- The baby's nervous system is overly sensitive to the outside world and receives too much stimulation.

When does colic occur?

The periods of turbulence occur two to three weeks after birth, and usually last until the third month or fourth month of the baby's life. It typically occurs between feedings in the afternoon.

How can I know that my baby is crying because of colic?

The baby cries a lot, is red in the face, nervously shifting her arms and legs. It's characteristic that the baby brings her legs to her stomach, tightens her fists, and enhances her activity. Screaming, which is sometimes completely inconsolable, can last for hours.

What should I do if my baby has colic?

If your baby is cries for a long time, it's necessary to examine if there are medical reasons for such intense crying (such as a painful middle ear or stuffy nose). If you suspect that it's not just colic, take the baby to the pediatrician.

If the baby is healthy and not hungry, thirsty, or wet, it's colic. The most important thing is to realize that it's a relatively common state that does not leave any consequences. You need to relax, keep a cool head, and not panic. Patiently await the end of this difficult period in your life.

What you can do:

1. Take the baby in your arms, gently swing or carry her around the house.

2. Wrap the baby in blankets to make her feel more secure and rock her in the stroller or cradle.

3. You can carry the baby in a carrier tightened to your chest. Babies like to feel the pounding of mom's heart, and that soothes them.

4. Some babies calm down while driving in a car, so you can take her for a drive around the neighborhood.

5. Massage her stomach, lubricated with warm baby oil.

6. Put a pre-warmed diaper on the baby's stomach and gently massage its sore tummy.

7. Give baby herbal tea that relieves pain from colic and breaks down gases.

8. Give the baby a calming syrup from the pharmacy. Do this exclusively according to the pediatrician's prescription, and only in the toughest cases.

9. Sing soothing songs to the baby, but quietly and close to her ear. She may be interested in the song and will stop crying to listen.

10. Check your diet if you are breastfeeding your baby. Avoid foods that can cause bloating (peas, beans, cabbage), and reduce the intake of carbonated drinks, coffee, chocolate, pepper, hot peppers, and other strong spices.

11. Leave her alone in the crib in a quiet room, with peaceful and soothing music (Mozart, Beethoven). She may calm down after a few minutes of crying.

Can colic cause complications if it lasts for a long time?

There won't be any complications. Babies with colic will be just as happy, smart, and well-adjusted as babies without colic. Even with colic, and despite hours of crying, babies progress perfectly and look healthy, gain weight, and grow in length.

How Babies' Senses Develop

How can a baby feel touch?

When a baby is born, the sense of the touch is as fully developed as in an adult. However, as the skin of your baby is very sensitive, she enjoys a gentle, warm touch the most. This resembles the warmth of the womb.

Since the skin of your newborn is very sensitive, you can influence the development of touch sensations with a mild massage along the whole body. Start exploring how your baby grows with your baby. Collect various materials such as cotton, silk, wool, and so on. Put them into your baby's hands one at a time and observe her reactions.

What kinds of tastes does the baby distinguish when it is born?

As soon as the baby is born, it can tell the difference between sweet and sour. Naturally, it is sympathetic to the sweet taste, so it's not surprising that breastmilk has a sweet taste. Recognizing salty flavors only develops after the fifth month.

When the baby is nine months old, it's time to introduce new flavors in nutrition, experts say. In this period, the development of taste is at its peak. The most important thing is to watch your baby's reactions while feeding. This way, you will easily discover which flavors she likes and which she doesn't.

What kind of scents do babies like?

When a baby is born it can distinguish several scents, and many like the smell of vanilla or banana. According to some studies, a baby can recognize the scent of its mother only a few hours after birth. Very quickly, babies develop an affection for certain scents. Experts claim that babies can recognize a breastfeeding woman by smell, and if they encounter two women who are breastfeeding, the baby prefers the scent of its mother.

As it grows, it's easier for a baby to recognize different scents. By the first year, most babies recognize the scents of adults other than their parents, as well as other children. They also begin to recognize the smell of different foods around this time, which can help you discover which foods your baby loves and which she doesn't.

How does the baby hear when it is born?

Babies react to the voices of adults, and they prefer quiet, calming tones. The only thing that babies can't hear is a whisper, while their sense of hearing has not been fully developed. During the first month, it will show interest in other voices and then explore its own voice.

The sense of hearing is very much related to speech. By the third month, your baby will make sounds and wait for you to answer. During this period, the baby can understand where the sound comes from, and by the seventh month, it will respond to its name.

How does a baby see when it is born?

During the first three months of life, the baby's visual field is limited to about eight to sixteen inches (twenty to forty cm). Everything beyond that is a blurred and irregular shape. It's not surprising that this is exactly the distance between the baby's face and the mother's during breastfeeding. Babies' attention is attracted by sharp contours and glittering objects.

In the first few months, you may notice that both of your baby's eyes do not focus at the same time. Don't worry, this is not a sign of strabismus. The baby's eye muscles will strengthen so that it can focus on a particular object or person. Also, the color of your baby's eyes will not be fixed until the end of the first year of life. Most babies are born with dark blue or gray eyes. The color of a baby's eyes can go through several changes before it is finally determined—usually somewhere between the third and the sixth month, and even longer for some babies.

Breastfeeding

Why is breast milk the best food for babies?

Mother's milk contains everything the baby needs in the first six months of life — nutrients, minerals, vitamins, water, and antibodies — literally, everything! Mother's milk improves the child's immunity and reduces the chance of the onset of illnesses later in life (allergies, asthma, various types of infections, diabetes, etc.). Children who were breastfed as babies have a lower risk of developing obesity, and also less need for dentures because their jaws and teeth develop better.

There are some studies that demonstrate a significant difference in the intelligence quotient of children who were breastfed compared to those who were not. The longer you breastfeed your baby, the more your baby will benefit from breast milk. If you are breastfeeding for more than four months, you reduce your baby's chance of getting an ear infection. Babies who have been breastfed for more than six months have a reduced risk of developing allergies.

Does breast milk have all of the necessary nutrients?

Yes, breast milk contains all that is needed for the development of a child for up to six months. It contains the ideal ratio of proteins, carbohydrates, fats, vitamins, and minerals, and there is no need to add any other ingredients, not even water. Baby gets enough of everything from mother's milk.

How does breastfeeding benefit me as a mother?

Breastfeeding is not only valuable for a baby. Immediately after delivery, breastfeeding helps to restore the uterus to its original size and makes postpartum bleeding shorter and lighter. Breastfeeding women rapidly return to their former weight, and some studies show that they have a lower risk of developing breast and ovarian cancer later in life.

In addition, breastfeeding is a much simpler way of feeding a baby — no bottles, sterilizers, bottle wash brushes, or milk boiling tubes. At night, it is much easier to nurse a baby than to prepare, shake, heat, and cool formula. Breastfeeding is free, while baby formula can be very expensive.

Does breastfeeding hurt?

If you do it right, it shouldn't hurt. It is possible that the breasts are more sensitive during the first few days when the milk is still beginning to come out and the baby isn't strong enough to suckle consistently. If the pain persists, it is likely that the baby doesn't latch on to the nipple properly and you need to try again and seek guidance to breastfeed correctly.

It can hurt if you have a wrinkle on your nipples. If you notice wounds that bleed on or around the nipples, be sure to contact your doctor or nurse.

What is colostrum?

Colostrum is the pale yellowish fluid that may leak from the breasts during pregnancy and in the first days after childbirth. It is the ideal food for your baby in the first days, and it's very dense and sticky, which makes it different from breast milk. It is a sort of concentrated milk. It's easy for a baby to digest and it doesn't provoke colic. It consists of water, proteins, and minerals in the ratio necessary for feeding. The most important ingredients in colostrum are antibodies that will protect the baby from infection. Colostrum is also a kind of laxative, and it helps to cleanse the baby's intestines from meconium, the baby's first stool.

Two to four days after childbirth, depending on your type of labor and whether it is your first or second baby, you will start producing "real" milk. While you are producing only colostrum, your breasts are not particularly big or tight. When you feel that they suddenly "overgrow," it's a sign that the colostrum is finished and the milk is coming.

How does breastfeeding benefit babies?

Breastfeeding primarily protects the baby from diarrhea, inflammation, respiratory infections, middle ear infections, and diabetes. Breastfed babies are less likely to suffer from asthma, allergies, eczema, and urinary tract infections; they have fewer dental problems and better vision. Heart disease can also be prevented by breastfeeding.

How do I breastfeed? Which position should I use?

You can breastfeed while sitting or lying down. In the first days after delivery, it is more comfortable if you nurse while lying down, because it is certainly not advisable to sit up for long stretches at a time. Lie down and place the baby along your side so that its stomach is next to yours. The most important thing is that the baby latches on to the breast correctly.

Later on, when you recover from labor and you and your baby get used to breastfeeding, this process will be extremely easy for you and you'll find the position that suits you the most.

How should I hold the baby so that it's breastfeeding properly?

Whether the baby lies down or is held in your arms, the most important thing is that she latches on correctly. Do not push the nipple into her mouth, but wait for her to touch the lower part of the areola with her lower lip and chin. It is very important for the baby to take the whole breast, so make sure that most of the areola is in her mouth.

How important is my nutrition during breastfeeding?

It's extremely important! You need to pay great attention to what you eat, perhaps even more than when you were pregnant. Keep in mind the fact that you are still continuing to feed your child, only now through the mammary glands (and not through the blood, as is the case during pregnancy).

I'm not sure if I'm getting enough nutrients — what are my needs?

Nutritional requirements are increased and depend on the amount of milk your glands secrete during the day (concerning the content of nutrients in milk). As your child grows and becomes more and more active, you have to satisfy her increased nutritional needs and make sure you are getting enough. If you look at the composition of your breast milk, you'll notice that you lose a significant amount of nutrients when it's excreted.

What is the chemical composition of breast milk?

Fats: 3.5%
Present in the form of fine emulsified drops, which are easy to digest and are more fully utilized. They are a significant source of heat energy and liposoluble vitamins A and D, and they add more unsaturated fatty acids (the amount of oleic acid is twice as high as in cow's milk). There's the most fat towards the end of the feeding.

Protein: 1.2 to 1.5%
Building material for new tissues and baby's growth. Most of the protein is caught in the infant tubes and goes into the blood where it serves for the growth and development of a young organism, while the smaller portion remains in the intestines and has a protective role.

Milk sugar (lactose): 7.2%
Present in twice the quantities of cow's milk.

Water: 87.5%
Comprises the highest percentage of the contents of breast milk. It is also lost during breastfeeding, so make sure to compensate by drinking plenty of water!

Minerals (salts of calcium, potassium, phosphorus — partly related to casein, and partly inorganic — magnesium, chlorine, sodium, sulfur): 0.2%

Mother's milk has all the minerals necessary for your infant up until the fifth month of life (from the fifth month on, the content in milk may be insufficient, especially in iron).

Vitamins: 0.3%

The vitamin content of breast milk depends on the mother's diet (if properly fed, the milk contains sufficient amounts of vitamins A, B, and C). There's not enough vitamin D naturally, so it has to be added to the food (adding vitamin D in supplements starts immediately after birth, and is best from the second week of life on — especially in the form of fish oil, which is rich in vitamin A as well).

Have my energy needs increased during the breastfeeding period?

Your energy needs have increased significantly compared to the pre-pregnancy period. It is necessary to "strengthen" your diet with an extra 300-500 calories a day (this is the amount of energy you can get from a slice of wheat bread, one boiled egg, and a cup of yogurt).

If you are breastfeeding twins, your energy needs grow by an additional 400-800 calories. Additional energy, in relation to the period before pregnancy, is necessary not only for breastfeeding, but also because of the changes to which your body is exposed (less sleeping, more activity, and so on).

You need about one ounce (20 gr) of protein a day, because you lose on average about .04 ounces (1.2 gr) of protein per 3.4 ounces (100 ml) of breast milk.

It is extremely important to take into account your calcium intake during breastfeeding (about 1,200 mg/day) because if you do not ingest sufficient amounts (food and supplements), the level of calcium in the milk will be maintained by pulling calcium from your tissue (primarily bone). If you are a vegetarian, take into account the importance of vitamin B12.

Zinc is also an essential mineral during breastfeeding, and recommendations are 15-20 mg daily. The source of zinc is eggs, meat, cereals (bread and wheat flour, flakes). With well-planned and combined foods, you will provide your body, and therefore your child (through the milk), with enough quantities of other minerals, too (the need is the same as during pregnancy).

Considering that about 87% of breast milk is water, it is necessary to compensate for this loss by drinking about six to twelve cups (1.5 to 3 liters) of liquid per day. (Tip: Drink four more glasses of water than you used to in the period before pregnancy.)

Bottle Feeding

What is supplementing with formula?

No milk can completely replace breast milk. It has been scientifically proven that breastfeeding has a positive effect on the health of you and your baby. We already talked about many benefits of nursing.

But in some cases, when a breastfed baby does not advance enough or when the mother does not have enough milk to satisfy her baby's appetite, the doctor may advise supplementing with formula. This means that the baby, besides breastfeeding, consumes infant formula from the bottle. The mother should not stop nursing or pumping milk, as it stimulates lactation. Breastfeeding should not be abandoned in these cases, because you should remember that your breast milk is healthier for your baby than any infant formula.

How can I know if I have enough milk and if I should supplement with formula?

Your doctor will answer this question. If the baby does not develop enough (as seen by body weight and length), or if she cries even after feeding, or if she sucks her fingers, your doctor may advise you to supplement with formula.

How can I bottle feed properly?

Prepare the baby for a meal

Keep the baby close to you in order to ensure that mealtime is relaxed, happy, and brings pleasure to both you and your baby. Being close and attached to a baby does not have to be linked exclusively to breastfeeding. Enjoy bottle feeding your baby.

Cuddling during feeding

Gently cuddle your baby's face to stimulate it to suck on the bottle. Talk to her softly, sing some soothing song. Make as much eye contact as you can. It is absolutely blissful for your baby to see you, hear you, and be fed at the same time.

Warming the milk

Some babies do not care if the milk is cold, but most prefer if it is warmed up to body temperature. Heat it by holding a bottle in hot water or using a bottle heater.

Sterilization

Gastroenteritis and other types of stomach problems are more common in bottle-fed babies, so be careful when it comes to hygiene. Regularly sterilize bottles, nipples, and protective caps.

The bottle's position

Have the bottle tipped downwards so that there is always milk in the nipple. This prevents the baby from swallowing too much air.

Caution: Never leave your baby alone while sucking from the bottle, because there is a risk of choking.

Rules for safe bottle feeding

In the past, bottle feeding involved a certain risk to the baby due to poor sanitary conditions, as well as the inadequate composition of baby formula. Babies did not progress well, they were susceptible to infections, were often ill, and even died. Today, it is quite different because there are high-quality milk formulas on the market. With certain hygienic measures and proper preparation, the health risks are almost non-existent.

Caution when shopping

Check the expiration date. Make it a habit to look at the production date of the item you are buying. Check the packaging. Avoid buying and using a formula that is in burnt, leaking, or otherwise damaged packaging.

Hygiene

- Wash your hands well before preparing the formula.
- Wash the lid with detergent and hot water before opening the can, rinse thoroughly, and dry.
- Open formula tins with a special can opener that you use exclusively for this purpose. After each use, wash the opener.
- Everything used to prepare a baby's meal should be washed in a special bowl only for that purpose. Sterilize the new object before use. After washing, rinse the soap from the bottles and nipples as well.
- Wash the bottles and nipples immediately after use with a special bottle brush to make cleaning easier.

Heating

- Heat the milk at the optimum temperature by placing the bottle in a hot water tank or using a bottle heater.
- Check the heat of the milk by placing it on your hand. It's ready for a baby if it's not hot nor cold.
- Do not reheat formula.
- Be cautious if you use a microwave oven for heating the milk — the liquid can heat unevenly and the bottle can be cold although the milk is boiling.

Storage

- Keep unadulterated formula in a cool, dark, dry place, or as indicated on the packaging.
- Throw away prepared formula that the baby did not finish. Already-prepared milk is an ideal environment for the development of bacteria.
- Do not dispose of formula at temperatures below 32°F (0°C) or higher than 95°F (35°C).
- Do not freeze the formula.
- Keep bottles with prepared formula in the refrigerator.

Bathing

What do I need for bathing my baby?

To bathe a newborn, besides a plastic tub and warm water, you need:

- a mild baby bath soap
- a jug of lukewarm water
- a bath sponge or cotton cloth for babies
- baby towel

Immediately after bathing, you will dress the baby and prepare her for sleep, so you need:

- baby diaper cream
- clean diaper, baby undershirt or body shirt, and sleeping bag or cotton clothes
- brush
- vitamin D solution (best to use it at bath time so you won't forget it)

How should I hold the baby while bathing her?

While the umbilical cord does not fall off, the baby should be bathed over the arm under a jet of water. Keep the baby over your forearm with a diaper covering the belly button. (While the umbilical cord does not dry up and doesn't fall off, a nurse may bathe the newborn.) Later, the baby is bathed lying on its back with head slightly raised, and also placed on the mother's forearm.

I'm afraid to bathe the baby because the umbilical cord has not fallen off yet. What can I do?

The baby should be bathed over the arm, under a jet of water. Hold the baby over the forearm, with a diaper on the baby's stomach. It's best to leave the umbilical cord wrapped. When the bathing is done, unwrap it and wipe it with the clean, sterile compress and povidone iodine two to three times. Always take a new sterile gauze to dry the umbilicus and wrap it again with sterile gauze.

What should I do if the baby cries during bathing?

Check if you have chosen the right time for bathing — she may be too tired and sleepy, or she's very hungry. Try one of these suggestions.

1. Move the bathing time to half an hour earlier and feed her a little.

2. Talk and smile at the baby while you are bathing her.

3. You may be nervous, in a rush, or you are too brusque and make sudden movements. Try to be gentler, more relaxed, sing while you are bathing her, or turn on some music.

4. Try to bathe together; the closeness and warmth of your body will relax the baby.

5. If she continues to cry too much while bathing, skip bathing for a few days and wash her only with a soaped sponge on the changing mat. Try again after two or three days and let your partner bathe her while you are assisting.

What is the correct bathing procedure?

Wash your hands and the tub before bathing.

Pour a little warm water into the tub and check the warmth of the water with your forearms. The depth of water should be about two inches (five cm). If you are not sure about the heat of the water, you can also check with a water thermometer. The temperature should be about 98°F (37°C).

Pour a little warm water into the jug. It will cool to the desired temperature while you bathe the baby.

Prepare everything you need for bathing. Keep everything in one place and at your fingertips (comb, bath soap, diaper cream, lotion, vitamin D, and cotton pads). Just add the baby's clean clothes and everything is ready.

Now, undress the baby. Take a cotton pad and wash your baby's eyes with clean water. Use new clean pads for each eye, and wipe it from the outside to the nose.

Put the baby slowly into the water. Talk to your baby and smile at her. Your left hand should be under the baby's shoulders. Her head is supported by your forearm. Your right hand is under the baby's bottom, and your right forearm supports her legs.

First, release your right hand by lowering the baby's bottom and legs into the water. Hold the child under the armpit with your left fingers. The baby's head rests on your left arm and never comes down entirely into the water. Hold the baby in a diagonal position so that the water reaches her chest. Your left hand is busy holding the baby's head while you are bathing her with your right hand.

Put a little bath soap into your right hand, wash baby's face first, then her head, neck, chest, stomach, genitals, then legs. Rinse off your hand or bath towel in the bathtub. The area of the genitals should be washed twice.

Turn the baby onto her stomach, holding the front of the chest and the head over your left hand, with her knees in the tub. Wash your baby's back, neck, bottom, and genitals.

Lift the baby over the tub and rinse her with clean water from the jug. Before this, check the temperature of the water in the jug with your hand. Rinse the baby from head to back, bottom, and legs. Then turn her over and rinse her from the front.

Take the baby out of the tub and wrap her in a large, soft towel. Instead of rubbing the baby, dry her with gentle tapping on the skin.

Wipe the baby's ears from the outside, apply the diaper cream and lotion, diaper the baby, dress her in clean clothes, give her vitamin D, and then pick her up. After bathing, babies always sleep longer, so it's nice to give her a bath in the evening when you and your partner have more free time.

Eight Tips for Safe Bathing

Bath time is a fun and special time you share with your baby. It's also a time to be particularly careful. Pay attention to these tips so your baby will be safe during bathing.

1. The first and most important rule is: Never, ever leave your baby unattended, even for a moment. Literally, everything is a potential danger – the water, a slipper, a towel, etc. If the phone rings or somebody comes to the door, wrap the baby in a towel and go together, or ignore it completely.

2. Warm the bathroom (approx. 75°F / 24°C), because the baby rapidly gets cold.

3. Do not put the baby in the tub as long as the water is on because the water pressure can change, it can quickly become colder or warmer than at first, or you can accidentally pour more than needed. First prepare enough water at the appropriate temperature and then put the baby in the tub.

4. Babies have very sensitive skin, so they prefer bathing in water that is not too hot, for newborns around 96°F (36°C) and for babies 98-100°F (37-38°C). You can test the water

with your wrist or elbow – it should be pleasantly lukewarm, not hot. If you can, get a special water thermometer.

5. Fill the tub only to about two to three inches (five to seven cm) for babies up to six months, and no more than the height of the hips (when in the sitting position) for the older child. Regardless of the small amount of water, the baby should never be left unattended, because it can drown in just a few inches of water.

6. Do not allow the child to touch the tap. Even if it's not able to move it for now, very soon it will be strong enough to turn the water on, which could be potentially very dangerous – especially if it happens to accidentally turn on hot water. (A good idea is to place the baby so the tap is behind its back during bathing).

7. Keep electrical appliances such as hair dryers, curling irons, or electric razors as far as possible from the tub.

8. Sometimes bathing can be very stressful because it happens at the end of the day when you are already tired. Additional care or assistance of another person or an older child is required because when you are tired, there are greater chances of accident or injury.

Does the baby have to bathe every day?

A frequent concern of new parents is how often a baby should be bathed. Some hold the point of view that babies should be bathed every day, while other studies show that newborns should be bathed once every four days because they don't get dirty enough to need daily bathing. Many agree that it's enough to bathe the baby twice a week, if you thoroughly clean the parts covered by diapers, or wash the baby's bottom every time she poops. Also, it's good to cleanse the body parts that are sweaty or dirty, such as behind the ears, under the armpits, and the neck.

Shampoos and soaps are intended to keep the particles of dirt and grease on the surface of the skin so that they can be easily removed by water. Without the use of soap with a certain degree of fat, dirt or surface secretions can adhere to the skin. In that case, their removal would require even stronger rubbing with water and a towel, which could irritate the skin.

Each baby has a different degree of tolerance to different shampoos or soaps. Baby skin, and especially the skin of newborns, is very sensitive. It is therefore important to use medicinal products designed exclusively for babies.

Should I use soaps and bubble baths?

You can bathe your newborn baby in clean water and add just a drop of olive or almond oil, or use the medicinal products for newborns.

If you use soap, follow the instructions. Namely, try it out on a small portion of the baby's skin. If the skin turns red, dries, or changes over other parts of the body in the next few hours, do not use that soap and try another one.

Always use mild soap, shampoo, or bubble baths with a neutral pH. Various baths and baby shampoos are in fact the same as those used for adults, but contain fewer supplements such as antibacterial substances, fragrances, or defoliants. Avoid hygiene products for adults.

Diapering a Baby

What do I need to diaper a baby?

The basic things you need to diaper a baby are:

- a diaper changing mat (or a thicker towel or blanket)
- absorbent cotton pads, lukewarm water, or a wet, soft towel for a baby under six weeks
- wet wipes for babies older than six weeks
- disposable diapers, swaddling bands, and a cotton napkin
- diaper cream
- spare clothes, in case the others get dirty
- something to dispose of used diapers.

Let everything be at your fingertips when you begin to diaper the baby. Never, ever leave your baby alone when changing it, even for a moment.

Where can I diaper my baby?

It's best to place the baby on a hard surface at waist level so that you don't have to hunch over. There are special dressers with changing boards on top, as well as specially designed baby changing boards that can be placed on the crib.

You can also diaper your baby on the washing machine in the bathroom, at a dresser of the appropriate height, or on the bed, if it's not difficult for you to sit while changing the baby. Later, you'll become so skillful that you'll be able to diaper the baby while in the stroller, car, or on special surfaces in the bathrooms of restaurants and supermarkets. The most important thing is to always use a special changing mat for that purpose.

What kinds of diapers exist?

There are several types of diapers. The most common are disposable diapers. They are easy to use, have a gelatin that absorbs moisture so the skin remains dry, and have adhesive tape that keeps them fixed in place.

Pros: They are easy to put on, convenient, and easy to use. After using, you just throw them away.

Cons: They are not ecological (the silicon they contain does not dissolve) and some babies may be allergic to the material they're made from. They are a more expensive solution, and as babies do not always have the feeling of being "wet," they find it harder to learn to use a toilet later.

Classic cotton tetra diapers are used alone or with paper inserts, usually held in place with plastic panties or swaddling bands. These diapers are more complicated to use because of washing and ironing. Cotton diapers should be washed at high temperatures after each use, and they are ironed for disinfection in the first six weeks.

Pros: They are ecologically correct, cheaper, have only one universal size, and they make it easier for a baby to get used to using the toilet.

Cons: They require washing, drying, and permanent disinfection by ironing. They don't have the absorption of the disposable ones, the baby's bottom is always wet, and it takes more time to change the baby.

How often should I change my baby and when?

As a rule, the baby should be changed before each feeding. In the first month, it's eight to ten times a day. Later, it's six to seven times a day. You shouldn't diaper her at night (from midnight to 5:00 a.m.), unless she is very wet or dirty.

Is your baby a sleeper? If a newborn is falling asleep while breastfeeding, it's convenient to change her after giving her one side and before starting the other. She will wake up, and then it's the right time to change her diaper. As the baby is still not full, she won't vomit and, most importantly, will continue feeding.

If you have noticed that your baby is pooping in the middle of feeding, wait until she is full and then diaper her. In this case, the baby should not be diapered before the feeding, and you will save time and diapers if you change her at the end of the feeding.

Soon you will know when it's best to diaper your baby: before feeding (according to regulation), during a feeding (sleepy one), or after a feeding (for babies who poop during feedings).

How many diapers do I need per week in the first six weeks?

The baby is changed at each feeding, so in the first six weeks, you will need about 70 diapers per week (eight to ten days). For all six weeks, you will need about 400 disposable wipes. If you are using cotton diapers, for the entire time of the baby's care, you will only need 60 to 70 diapers total (that can be washed in a washing machine).

Where is the best choice of diapers?

You will soon be a real expert on stock diaper sales. Cloth diapers are purchased in specialized baby equipment stores, and the disposable ones you can find in almost all pharmacies, grocery stores, drug stores, and discount supermarkets.

Buy the largest package of disposable wipes because they are the most cost-effective. It's important that you do not allow yourself to get caught at night or on holidays and weekends without diapers. When shopping, make sure the package is not damaged. There must not be any breaks or holes through which dust or impurities could enter.

How should I wash cotton diapers, and can I use a softener?

During the day, collect used cotton diapers in a bucket filled with water, laundry powder, and stain whitener. (A diaper dirty with baby poop should be rinsed under a jet of water first before being placed in the bucket with other diapers.)

When you collect enough diapers, which is usually about 25 at the end of the day (eight to ten diaper changes per two diapers, plus a few for wiping), you can add a bath towel and a few body-shirts, and you have a full washing machine.

Always choose a program for washing white laundry at high temperatures with pre-wash and boiling water. Once the machine is finished, it is usually best to flip the rinsing cycle one more time. It's better to use water softener than a fabric softener. You have to disinfect the baby's clothes by ironing them for the first six weeks. Always do baby's laundry separately from yours.

Diapering Procedure

1. Wash your hands with soap and water. Never change a baby if your hands aren't entirely clean.

2. Place a changing mat where you are going to diaper the baby (a changing table when you are at home, a car seat, a sofa, an armchair when you are visiting, a washing machine if you are in the bathroom, a special area in restaurant bathrooms). You can use a special mat for that purpose, a thick towel, or a plain, clean cotton tetra diaper.

3. Put the baby on this mat, unfasten her clothes, and pull them towards her head so you can change the diaper. Make this procedure fun for the baby, talk to her and smile.

4. Unwrap the cotton diaper or peel the straps on the side of a dirty disposable diaper.

5. Always check the diaper's contents — the stool should be formed, golden yellow, without mucus or blood. The urine should not sting.

6. Take the diaper front and wipe the groin and baby's bottom. The baby must be wiped from top to bottom. Wrap the dirty diaper so that the front part is swung across the back and tape the strap to keep the contents inside. Wrap it like a packet and throw it in the trash. Use wet wipes, a clean damp cloth, a wet towel, or a wet cotton swab to wipe the baby's genitals, groin, bottom, and all creases.

7. Wipe girls from the front to the back and do not use the same wet wipe or damp cotton the other way. Repeat the procedure with a new wipe and, remember, always from the front to the bottom, never the opposite direction.

8. Wipe boys clean of feces and quickly cover the penis with a spare diaper to avoid being "showered" if he pees again.

9. To make sure the baby's bottom is well-wiped, lift the baby's both legs with your left hand. Wipe here once again with your right hand.

10. When the baby is completely clean, take a new clean diaper. Re-lift the baby's legs with one hand, and with another, place a clean diaper under the baby.

11. Place diaper cream on baby's bottom, genitals, and groin. Lift the diaper front (usually there are some colorful details) and connect the front and back of the diaper using sticky strips that are on each side.

12. Check that you have tightened your baby's stomach or legs by passing your finger between the diaper and the baby's body. Make sure that the straps are not stuck to the baby's skin.

13. Do not forget to talk to the baby, smile at her, cuddle, and kiss her during this process.

14. At the end of the procedure, place the baby in the crib, throw the dirty diaper in the trash, and wash your hands thoroughly.

Caring for Your Newborn's Umbilical Cord Stump

How to take care of the baby's umbilical cord stump?

The umbilical cord is cut and bound at birth. Upon leaving the maternity ward, an umbilical cord stump is usually seen. This dries up and disappears at about the tenth day of life. In the first few days after returning home, the baby's navel should be taken care of by a nurse. She should show you how to do it and will introduce you to the basic things that you need to know to prevent an infection of the umbilical cord.

Procedure

1. Unwrap the bandage from the navel and throw it away.

2. Take a sterile compress and soak it with povidone iodine.

3. Clean up the umbilical cord wound with povidone iodine.

4. Throw away the used gauze and take another, soaked with povidone iodine.

5. Clean the area with povidone.

6. Repeat everything once again.

7. Put a dry compress on the navel and turn it over to wrap or twist it with a larger sterile gauze (ask your nurse to show you how).

If the navel leaks fluid, or has an adjacent reddening granule, or a whitish growth (like a small white cauliflower), you should take the baby to a pediatrician.

What can I use for treating the baby's navel?

For navel care, povidone iodine is adequate. The antiseptic (yellow) powder is no longer used, and 3% hydrogen is used by pediatricians and nurses in cases of infection or appearance of granulomas.

How long does it take for the umbilical cord stump to fall off?

This is relative. In some babies, this happens in three days and in others, not two weeks. All umbilical cord stumps that do not drop in two weeks should be examined by a pediatrician. Do not try to pull the stump or remove it in any way. When it's dry, it will fall off. When this happens, a wound will appear that has to be treated for a few more days.

If the stump does not fall off in time, what's the reason?

There is a possibility that the baby has fistulas (small canals that connect the bladder), or that there is an infection that the pediatrician will recognize and properly treat.

Can complications occur if the umbilical cord stump is not maintained properly?

Yes, there may be complications. The most common is the redness around the navel, then the unpleasant odor, and the appearance of secretion when the navel leaks fluid. You should immediately contact a doctor who will, in addition to local care, also determine antibiotic therapy for your baby. As soon as you notice redness or that the navel is leaking, contact a doctor immediately, as these are signs of infection and need to be treated in time.

My baby's umbilical cord stump dropped off, but the wound still leaks. What should I do?

After the umbilical cord falls off, there might still remain a part of the inflamed tissue that leaks. Doctors claim that this is not a cause for concern and this phenomenon is very common and completely harmless. Take the baby to the doctor, and he will clean the inflamed part of the umbilicus with a stick of soaked silver-nitrate. The procedure is effective and painless for the baby.

What is an umbilical hernia?

It is a painless growth around the navel. In a large number of cases, neither therapy nor surgery is needed because it disappears by the second year of the baby's life. If the hernia does not retract by the baby's third year, doctors will most likely surgically remove it.

Baby Nail Care

Are there special accessories for baby nail care?

Yes. There are special flat-top scissors and nail clippers for babies. Be sure to buy new accessories that you will only use for her — do not use the scissors or clippers of your older child or adults.

My baby was born with long nails. When can I cut them?

Babies are often born with long nails that bother them because they unconsciously scratch their face. However, you should not cut her nails until she reaches two weeks. To avoid the scratching, use special gloves for newborns.

How do I trim baby nails correctly?

Nails should be trimmed once a week in the following way:

1. Wash your hands with soap and water.

2. Sit the baby in your lap (if she is very restless, you can cut her nails while she is asleep). The best time for manicures and pedicures is after bathing.

3. Wipe the scissors and baby's nails with alcohol.

4. Press the fingertip to separate it from the nail.

5. Hold the baby's hand with one hand, and cut the nails using another one.

6. Nails should be cut straight.

Baby Mouth Hygiene

I noticed some whiteness in my baby's mouth. What is it?

It is most likely oral thrush, a common fungal infection. Although it's usually harmless, it can cause many problems in the baby's mouth. The baby could "pick it up" in the birth canal. It is caused by a fungus, *Candida albicans*, a regular resident of the vagina and mouth.

The thrush appears as white spots or patches in the baby's mouth. You may see it inside baby's cheeks, on your baby's gums, on their tongue, or the palate (the roof of their mouth). Unlike pieces of milk, the patches do not wash or rub off easily. The tissue underneath will be red and raw. Although the patches are harmless, your baby may be reluctant to feed if they are sore. Place a sterile gauze on your finger and dip it in a solution of soda-bicarbonate and water, and then scrub the baby's palate, tongue, and inside cheeks gently.

Most cases of oral thrush clear up in a few days without any treatment. If symptoms persist or they are particularly difficult, ask your pediatrician or nurse for advice, or visit your doctor. Several antifungal gels or drops can treat oral thrush. However, some of them are not suitable for very young babies, so don't forget to speak to your doctor or pharmacist before you use them.

If the baby is breastfeeding, the mother's nipples should be treated at the same time as the baby to prevent the infection from passing back and forth.

The baby has small white swelling on the gums. Is this dangerous?

No. Believe it or not, those are the baby's teeth. Some babies have their teeth close to the surface. The other possibility is that they are small cysts or fistulas filled with liquid. Such cysts are common and will soon disappear without any problems, and your baby's gums will soon be clean and pink.

My newborn has yellowish white spots on the palate. Should I worry?

The yellowish-white spots on the gums of the newborn are known as Epstein pearls. These stains are also pretty common. There are no medical reasons for their appearance. Don't worry, they will soon disappear.

Baby's Ears and Eyes

Can I clean my baby's ears with cotton swabs?

Never place a stick or anything else in your baby's ear canal. You could easily break through the baby's eardrum. Wax is a natural protection of the ear canal and there is usually no need to clean it.

If you are concerned about the increased amount of wax in the baby's ears, consult a doctor. If so much wax has accumulated that the doctor cannot see the eardrum (which must be done when the ears are checked for infection), then the doctor will remove it. Otherwise, the wax will eventually come out. If you use a cotton swab, you will only push the wax deeper into the baby's ear.

Instead, just clean the outer parts of the baby's ears by applying a little oil on a wad of cotton or moisten a soft cloth with warm water.

Why are my baby's eyes always watery and sticky?

If a baby's eyes are watery and sticky, this means that the baby has an infection. If the mother had vaginal secretion or bacteria in the urine, it is probable that the baby caught the infection while going through the birth canal. In that case, the baby's eyes are red, swollen, and sticky, not only in the morning but throughout the day. It would be best to visit a doctor.

How do I wipe my baby's eyes?

If you notice just a slight change, wash the baby's eyes with chamomile tea a few times a day. Dip a clean, sterile gauze into lukewarm chamomile tea, and wipe the eyes from the outside to the nose. Repeat the procedure three to four times, using a new, sterile gauze each time. It is essential to clean the eyes from the outside to the inside, and that one gauze or wad is not used for another eye.

I can't determine the color of my baby's eyes. Is that normal?

Until it's a year or so old, the favorite entertainment of a family with a new baby is guessing the color of her eyes. Most babies are born with dark blue or gray eyes. The color of the baby's eyes can go through several changes before it's finally determined, somewhere between the third and the sixth month, and even longer for some babies. The color of the baby's eyes will not be final until the end of the first year, as the pigmentation of the iris increases throughout the first year.

My baby is cross-eyed. Will this change?

In the first couple of months, you may notice that the baby's eyes do not work in harmony, but it's not a sign that your baby has strabismus. Baby has not yet mastered the use of her eyes and the eye muscles are probably still strengthening. When she is three months old, she will probably be able to focus her eyesight.

If, however, you are quite sure that the baby uses only one eye when focusing on something, and the other looks somewhere random, ask for a doctor's advice. React in time, because ignoring this problem can cause semi-blindness or eye laziness.

When my baby cried during the first few days, there were no tears; now she cries like a rainy day. What's going on?

Tears appear before the end of the first month of life. Before that, newborns cry without tears. Only when the organism starts to produce this salty liquid using tear glands will your baby begin to cry "normally" (with tears). This liquid flows through the channels known as tear ducts that are located in the inner part of both eyes and the nose.

Since recently, my baby always looks as if she were crying even when she laughs. Why?

In one out of a hundred babies, one or both tear ducts can be blocked at birth. Since they are blocked, they can't empty, and there are always tears in the eyes. That's why your baby seems to have teary, wet eyes, even when she is happy and laughs. This problem will resolve itself by the end of the first year.

My baby is bleary-eyed in the morning. What should I do?

When the tear ducts are blocked, especially in the morning, a large amount of yellowish-white mucus is accumulated. The baby's eyelids can even get stuck together. It is best to clean them with cold boiled water, using sterile gauze. There's no need to worry or get nervous if there's no serious quantity of dark-yellow colored mucus, or if the white of the eye turns red. In that case, it is best to contact a doctor, who should prescribe antibiotic cream or drops.

Washing Baby Clothes

Baby clothes should always be washed separately from the rest of the family's clothes.

Colored clothing is most often washed at 104°F (40°C), and white fabrics at 140°F (60°C). For diapers, bedding, and towels, choose a program for washing white laundry at high temperatures 194 °F (90°C) with prewash. Once the machine has finished washing, you can turn on the rinse option again.

Clothes that are newly bought can be washed at 86°F (30°C), only to remove the dust that collects when the clothes are on the rack for a long time.

Are there any washing machines with a special baby cycle?

There are washing machines with a special baby cycle. The baby cycle allows you to wash clothes at a temperature of over 194°F (90°C). In this way, you achieve the maximum level of hygiene for the baby's clothes. Some washing machine manufacturers also offer the option of locking the machine's display so that children cannot change the washing cycle out of curiosity.

Which detergent should be used?

Baby skin is very sensitive and can react very dramatically to certain substances that laundry detergents contain. When washing is done, check if the clothes are "sticky." If this is the case, they were not washed well, and it would be a good idea to switch on the rinse cycle again.

Is it permitted to use a baby fabric softener?

The skin of newly born babies is extremely sensitive. It can react to the detergent, but also to the softener. This can cause allergies that occur in the form of redness, rash, swelling of the skin, itching, or even respiratory irritation.

However, if you want your baby's clothes to be soft and smell nice, get special softeners that are designed for sensitive skin. Actually, they are specifically designed for washing baby clothes. Usually, such softeners have a very mild fragrance because they contain fewer perfumes, but make the clothes softer and gentle to the touch.

You need to be very careful when buying a fabric softener. To avoid any unpleasant allergic reactions on your child's skin, avoid the softeners which are not marked as safe for use from the earliest age.

What should I look for when buying detergent and softener?

When purchasing detergent and softener to wash your baby's clothes, make sure they have a mild, gentle scent, are biodegradable, and contain natural additives. Also, there should be an indication on the package that proves they have been dermatologically tested on sensitive skin, and the 0+ mark, which means that they can be used from the youngest age, practically from birth.

Baby and Winter

If you live on a tropical island, you can skip this part. But if you live on a part of the globe where there are four seasons, you'll want to know a few dos and don'ts regarding a baby and winter.

Should we take the baby outside in the winter?

Although grannies from your neighborhood probably would not agree with us, you must take your baby out to get fresh air every day, starting from the second week after leaving the maternity ward.

Babies born in winter require a little more care, and should wait to go out until they are a month old. The length of the time spent outside should be gradually increased day by day, thus getting the child used to fresh air.

Low temperatures are not obstacles for walking until the temperature drops below 14°F (−10°C). The only obstacles in winter are wind, rain, snow, fog, and snow storms.

Since it's the warmest around noon during the wintertime, try to synchronize the baby's rhythm with it and take a walk every day around noon.

Taking a walk with mom and dad, or with grandparents, improves the general condition of the child, as fresh air affects her appetite, sleep, mood, and the resistance to infection.

During the walk, the baby learns about sounds, objects, is introduced to the environment, meets the outside world, and others meet her, too.

How do I dress my baby for winter?

Since the body of children under two years is difficult to adapt to low temperatures and rapidly cools, a baby should be warmly dressed in with multilayered clothes.

A baby winter suit is always welcome because it safely protects the baby's back. A hat, scarf, and gloves are an essential part of winter wear. Also, a baby should wear warm boots for snow. If your child has already learned to walk, then the boots should be waterproof.

If your child is already walking and enjoying the snow, you should change her clothes immediately if she gets wet and is not wearing waterproof gear. Tip: It's smart to tie the gloves to a woolen thread and slide them through the sleeves of the winter suit so that you do not lose them.

As a rule, the child should be dressed the same way as the parents. Still, even if the outdoors are just a bit cool, the baby should wear a hat.

If the temperature is around zero, the baby's ears must be covered with a hat, the hands with gloves, and the neck with a scarf. When it's windy, a baby should wear a scarf. Baby's face can also be wrapped, but the nose must not be blocked.

Be sure to take a protective cover for strollers and a slicker, so you can protect the baby in case of bad weather. Likewise, if it gets warmer during a walk, you can take off one of the layers of clothing.

When you enter a warm place, even for a few minutes, take off the baby's jacket or winter suit. You have to be careful not to warm the baby too much because it can cause heat shock. Experts claim that warming a baby too much in the winter months, when flu and other respiratory infections are the most prevalent, can lead to sudden infant death syndrome (SIDS).

How much time should we spend in the fresh air in the wintertime?

It depends on the outside temperature. If the temperature is low, even a well-wrapped baby should not stay out for a long time.

If the baby's hands are warm, and the baby is obviously feeling well, this means that you can still stay in the fresh air.

If the baby's hands are cold, and she becomes cranky or is in a bad mood, she's probably had enough of being in the fresh air (unless she's hungry, thirsty, or has pooped) and you need to take her back to the warmth of home. If she starts to cry, you definitely should finish the walk.

Do not be confused if a baby's nose runs when you're in the cold; when you enter a warm place, it should stop.

Does baby's skin need special care in the winter?

Baby skin can become dry and chapped in the wind. For this reason, use a fatty and moisturizing baby skin cream.

If the baby uses a pacifier, or if she's teething and drools, the cheeks must be wiped from time to time so that the skin does not get chapped.

If you go on vacation somewhere in the mountains to enjoy the snow, the child should use protective sunglasses and sunscreen with a high UV factor. For choosing and using protective sunscreen, consult your pediatrician. Like adults, not all babies have the same type of skin.

Soap and chemicals dry out the skin, so they should be used more moderately in the winter. After bathing, do not rub the baby's skin, just dry it by patting it with a towel so that you do not irritate the dry skin.

It is desirable to moisten the air in the baby's room during the winter months to make it easier for the baby to breathe.

What dangers can threaten my baby in the winter?

You need to be seriously concerned if your baby's nose, ears, faces, or toes become very cold and turn yellowish-gray color. This indicates frostbite and can cause serious injury.

In this case, the baby needs to be warmed up. First unbutton your coat or jacket and hug your baby to raise her body temperature with your body temperature. Then, as soon as possible, go to your doctor or emergency service.

If you are not able to reach the doctor urgently, try to warm your baby home, but not suddenly, as this can worsen the situation.

The frozen part of the body should be heated in water that is warmed slightly above average body temperature, no higher than 102°F (39°C) – be sure to use a thermometer! Or you should use a compress at the same temperature, but don't put added pressure on it.

It is necessary to use compresses until the skin gets back its standard color. Breastfeed the baby or give her a warm (not hot) drink.

If the baby's skin gets red, blisters, or becomes swollen, it's time for a doctor to see her. It would be best if he could visit you at home, so you do not have to bring your baby out into the cold air again.

Teething

When will my baby get her first teeth?

Most often, the first tooth appears when the baby is six months old. It is the lower central tooth (central incisor), and the second lower central incisor comes after it. When they start to grow, new teeth appear every month, so your baby will have about six teeth by her first birthday.

What is the normal growth dynamic of baby teeth?

First, the baby will have four central (two lower and two upper incisors) when she is six to seven months old. Then there are four lateral incisors in the period of about eight months. Four molars appear from the tenth to fourteenth month, and after them, you can expect four canines, from the sixteenth to the twentieth month. The last four molars will grow in the period from 24 to 30 months.

This order and the time of the occurrence of teeth are the golden averages, as all babies differ. Some babies still have no teeth at a year, while there are even babies who are born with a tooth or two.

My ten-month-old baby still does not have any teeth. Is everything all right with her development?

Unlike physical growth and development, tooth growth does not depend on whether the baby is well-fed and whether she's healthy – teeth appear at the right moment. For some babies, the first tooth does not grow in until the first birthday, but that does not mean that they are behind in their development.

If you visit a dentist, you will see that teeth already exist in the baby's jaw and will appear in time.

My baby had a tooth when she was born. Should this tooth be removed?

A small number of babies are born with a tooth in a jaw. If the tooth is loose, it must be taken out so that the baby will not swallow it. A gap at the site of the tooth will remain until the growth of permanent teeth by school age. But if the so-called natal tooth is solid, it should not be a problem.

How do I differentiate between the symptoms of disease and teething?

Symptoms of tooth growth are usually mild. However, babies in the sixth month begin to lose the immunity inherited from their mothers. As teeth begin to grow during this period, it often happens that babies get sick. Parents are able to underestimate the symptoms of disease and attribute them to teething, but be careful. If the baby has a fever or an unusual cry, take her to a doctor.

How do I know that my baby has started teething?

In general, there should be no major problems in the growth of teeth until the molars begin to grow. The baby may experience some of the following symptoms:

- A slight increase in temperature – this can occur immediately before the tooth's appearance. If the baby gets a fever, visit a doctor.
- The baby will probably be moody. She won't sleep well and will require extra care for a night or two. But if she is continually crying, don't hesitate to get in touch with a doctor.
- Babies' gums may look dark pink and slightly swollen.

My baby puts everything in her mouth. Does this mean that teething has begun?

The baby's chewing of everything is not a sign that her teeth are growing in, say most experts who consider this process as a stage in the child's oral development.

Is the redness on my baby's cheeks connected with teething?

Like putting everything in her mouth, the red rash on the baby's cheeks has nothing to do with teething. Experts believe that this redness is caused by one type of virus.

How can I alleviate the problems associated with teething?

- Give the baby a crust of bread to chew.

- It can help, and it's fun, chewing a special rubber ring that has been previously cooled in the fridge. The cold will relieve pain in her gums. (Don't try to sweeten the ring!)

- Apply a special gel to the baby's gums with a clean finger. The gel will gently calm painful gums.

- If the baby cannot calm down, give her a dose of paracetamol for babies.

- If all of this fails, contact your doctor.

How can I prevent cavities?

A healthy diet during pregnancy and breastfeeding ensures that baby teeth are firm. The best drink for your baby in the period of tooth growth is breast milk. When buying baby beverages, be sure to check the content of lactose, fructose, and other forms of sugar. Avoid giving babies sweetened or carbonated drinks, as they can damage the teeth.

What you should not do:

- Do not get the baby used to drinking sweetened drinks before bedtime or during the night.

- Do not lull her to sleep or comfort her with a sweetened drink or pacifier.

- Always look for medicines without sugar.

Do I brush my baby's teeth and when should I start?

As soon as the first tooth appears, it can be brushed. Introduce the baby to tooth brushing, and get her used to maintain the hygiene of her teeth and mouth as early as possible. Buy a specially designed toothbrush for babies. Brush her teeth at least once a day.

Do I use toothpaste when brushing my baby's teeth?

Hold back on the toothpaste until the baby learns to spit the fluid from her mouth.

How can I clean baby teeth?

- Take the baby's head in your hands.

- At the beginning (while the baby still doesn't have any teeth), it will be most convenient for you to use a piece of clean gauze wrapped around your forefinger. Later you can use a small, soft toothbrush.

- Gently massage the gums and teeth with a brush.

- When a child grows a bit and wants to brush her teeth by herself, let her do it, but show her how to do it right (up and down, not from left to right).

Do I need to give my baby fluoride supplements?

Although fluoride helps to strengthen the teeth, too much fluoride can also have a damaging effect and there may be a loss of tooth color. It would be best if you consult with your dentist how much fluoride you should give to the baby and at what age should you start.

Skin Care

Which products do I need for baby skin care?

It is very important that before buying, you check whether the collection you want to purchase is suitable for the sensitive skin of the baby. You need bath soap, a very mild shampoo, a fatty baby cream for the diaper area, and optionally a powder.

Will the soap damage the skin of my baby?

No, but it can make skin dry. If you notice dryness, apply baby cream or lotion to the baby's skin from head to toe after bathing.

Do I use wet wipes if they irritate the skin of my baby?

If you notice that wet wipes irritate her skin, reduce their use to a minimum. Use them only when you are not able to wash the baby's bottom with soap and water (when you are on the trip or out of the house). You can try out wipes that are not wet but oiled, which greatly clean and nourish the baby's skin.

Should I put cream on my baby's face?

Try to apply cream to the baby's face as little as possible. Apply a little after bathing, before bedtime. The baby's face should be protected from cold and dry air and from strong sunshine.

How to nourish the baby hair and skin on the head?

The hair and skin of the newborn's head are washed with a mild shampoo that is suitable for the newborn. When bathing, shampoo your baby's hair twice, rub it, and rinse. You should not be afraid, the fontanelle is soft, and the skin of the head moves up and down, but it cannot be damaged by rubbing. When the baby is bathed and dried with a towel, brush the hair with a soft brush.

What is cradle cap?

Cradle cap is a common name for the seborrheic dermatitis of the head—greasy, yellowish deposits on the scalp.

What is the cure for cradle cap?

Around noon, pour some oil into the baby's hat and put it on her head. Don't take it off until evening. After evening bathing, rub the head with a towel and brush the hair with a thick comb. Repeat the procedure until you completely get rid of cradle cap. You need to be persistent because it can take a few days.

Why does cradle cap appear?

Cradle cap occurs in children who have a predisposition to it, and they are usually more prone to eczema, allergies, asthma, and bronchitis later. It gets worse when the head sweats, so make sure it does not overheat. Put on the baby's hat only when it's necessary.

How often should I wash my baby's hair?

It's enough to wash baby hair two to three times a week. If the baby's hair is greasy due to a sleeping hat or extremely oily skin, then shampoo it more often.

How should I shampoo the baby's hair?

1. Wet the baby's head with a mild jet from a cup. Put a drop of baby's shampoo on your palm to make a foam, and then shampoo the baby's hair.

2. While shampooing your baby, make sure that the shampoo does not enter your baby's eyes.

3. Rinse the baby's hair with a mild jet or with two or three cups of lukewarm water.

4. As you are rinsing your baby's hair, prevent the water with the shampoo from getting into the baby's eyes. It is best to put your hand on your baby's forehead to protect her eyes.

Skin Problems

Why is newborn skin more sensitive?

The skin of newborns and babies is gentler than in adults due the sensitive surface layer and thinner subcutaneous tissue. There is also less lipid content and more water than in the skin of grown-ups. Also, sebaceous glands and sweat glands are not fully developed, and the thermoregulatory mechanism is also sensitive. These are all factors that make the skin more easily drained and susceptible to infection. Particularly sensitive is the diaper region where unwanted changes occur frequently.

What causes unwanted changes in the skin?

- Heat, moisture, and lack of air in impermeable diapers increase the risk of irritation and most often lead to redness.

- Constant rubbing of the diaper on the skin can cause redness and even wounds.

- Hygiene with inappropriate washing and care products that can disrupt the pH of the skin and excessively dry the baby's skin can cause redness and pain.

- Urine and stool may affect the pH of the skin and lead to damage to the surface layer. Enzymes, bacteria, and fungi also contribute to this.

- Washing cotton diapers at lower temperatures is not advised as detergents, soaps, and softeners can cause inflammation or worsen existing conditions.

Although she's only two weeks old, my baby's skin has red streaks with a white center. What is this?

Newborns rarely have perfect skin. A widespread "cosmetic" problem of newborns is toxic erythema. Though it looks terrible on the skin of newly born babies – a blotchy red rash with small bumps that can be filled with fluid – this phenomenon is benign and temporary. No therapy is needed. Within a few days, your baby will look perfect.

My baby has tiny pimples all over her face. What should I do?

You were staring at the baby's face to find out who the new family member looked like and saw the small white "heads" around the nose, the chin, and even a few on the arms and stomach. These white spots are called milia. Almost half of newborns have them. They are caused by the plugging of the immature sebaceous glands. Also, excess sebum can cause them and they can also be a consequence of the flow of hormones through the placenta in the last few months of pregnancy. The best medicine is to do nothing. Resist the temptation to squeeze or rub them out. The spots should disappear on their own, without treatment, in a few weeks.

I noticed a rash in the diaper area. What should I do?

Your best friends are water and air, namely bathing and airing. Leave the baby without a diaper on for some time, as often and as long as you can. That will allow the air to circulate over the part of her body that is always covered with a diaper.

In case of diaper rash, change the diaper more frequently. Wash the baby each time she pees, and especially when she poops. The rash should not last longer than two days.

My baby has small blisters in the folds of her skin. What are they?

These small blisters occur due to the blocking of the sweat glands and disappear after a few days. You may have warmed your baby too much. Remove one layer of clothing or regulate the temperature of the bathing water.

What are the tiny red dots on my baby's face?

This phenomenon on the baby's skin may be an allergic reaction to excessive heat. This allergy often appears in summer, although it can also occur in the winter if your home is too warm. The dots will be disappear by themselves, and you shouldn't let the baby get too warm.

My baby has red stains above the level of the skin that itches. What could they be?

These can be symptoms of urticaria or hives, other skin allergies. The most common causes of allergies are food, soaps, and medicines. To soften the welts and soothe the itch, cover the area with a cool cotton diaper and lubricate it with a calamine-based cream. If the rash spreads, contact your doctor.

My baby's skin has started to peel. Is that normal?

Yes, skin peeling usually occurs around the wrists and toes, and indicates dryness of the skin. Put more baby lotion or body milk on those parts of the skin, and bathe the baby in clean water without shampoo.

My baby has some kind of rash on her skin. Is it dangerous?

If you notice any kind of rash, consult with a nurse first. If the rash does not disappear even after regular bathing and changing, consult with the doctor. He will identify the kind of rash and determine the treatment. In the case of a rash, it is necessary to determine which kind of rash it is.

Allergic rash
There is an allergic rash that occurs immediately after delivery and looks like hives. This rash does not need to be cured because it quickly disappears without any treatment.

Infectious rash
This kind of rash is usually caused by fungal candidiasis. In this case, antibiotics and antiseptics should be used. This rash occurs in the diaper area where the baby's skin is in contact with feces. It is manifested by red spots that are easily recognized by doctors and pediatric nurses.

Viral rash
There is also a viral infection that can cause a rash. This is not easily treated and occurs if the mother has herpes. If she still has herpes on her mouth, she must wear a mask.

Why is my baby's skin so dry?

The skin of a baby or a child can be as dry as adults' skin. But since young skin is more sensitive, it is more likely to be dry.

Cold outside air, as well as heating, can dry out the skin during winter. If the child's skin is prone to drying, it is likely that the dryness will also occur during the summer due to strong sunshine, air conditioning of the enclosed space, salt water, and chlorinated water in the pool. All of this also affects the drying of the skin.

What can I do to alleviate the symptoms of dry skin?

Bathing dries out the baby's skin, as it removes the natural protective layer of fat and dirt from the skin's surface. However, if you take precautions, even daily bathing should not be a problem.

Instead of half-hour bathing, shorten the time to ten minutes. Use warm water, not hot, and mild bath soaps for sensitive skin.

Let the baby play in the water before bathing, so she will spend less time in the soap. Also, reduce the amount of soap you use.

What problems does dry skin indicate?

If you notice red patches on your baby's skin, it is possible that it is eczema, specifically, atopic dermatitis. It is possible to solve the problem with regular daily skin care, so you don't have to rush to the doctor. Be sure to seek advice if changes in the skin do not disappear fast.

Sometimes dry skin may indicate a genetic condition known as ichthyosis. Ichthyosis is manifested by redness and thickening of the skin. Follow-up signs are also thickening in the palms and heels. Consult your doctor, and if there is any suspicion that may be ichthyosis, you will need to consult a dermatologist.

How do I use lotion?

As soon as you complete the bath and take the baby out of the tub, dry her with a towel and apply the appropriate lotion immediately. This way, the skin will retain the extra moisture that it needs, as it is kept within the skin after bathing. If the baby's skin is still dry, try using lotion twice a day: once after bathing and once again during the day.

Do I need to consult a doctor for dry skin?

When you go to a regular pediatric appointment with your child, ask for advice on how to fight dry skin. Be sure to schedule a special appointment if you see signs of eczema or ichthyosis. Also, schedule an evaluation if, despite regular skincare, you don't notice improvement or there are signs of infection.

How can I protect my child's skin from artificial matter?

The skin of the newborn is more susceptible to the harmful effects of artificial agents than adult skin. This is why the risk of systemic poisoning is much higher in newborns.

Experts warn that factors that affect the occurrence of rashes include skincare products for babies. If you read the packaging on a baby skincare product, you may find that some of them contain ingredients that can be contaminated with formaldehyde, 1.4-dioxanes, and even nitrosamine. These are ingredients that can cause cancer, severe skin irritation, or both.

Children's talc-based powders contain fine particles that can irritate the skin and may contain perfumes, the leading cause of allergies and irritation. It's a good idea to avoid children's talc powders.

For the care of children's skin, it's best to use products without artificial colors and synthetic fragrances. Look for products that have a pH balance with natural herbal extracts and essential oils. Skin care products that help alleviate irritation can be further enriched with vitamins.

What healing herbs can help?

Calendula has anti-inflammatory and antimicrobial characteristics, and also stimulates skin cell renewal.

Aloe vera helps to restore tissue integrity and has mitigating anti-inflammatory, antioxidant properties.

Chamomile prevents the release of histamine and relieves inflammatory response. It also stimulates the regeneration of the skin cells.

Almond works very well to maintain the necessary moisture of the skin. It protects against irritation and drying.

What are the benefits of vitamins?

Vitamin A is needed for the growth and restoration of body tissue and helps maintain skin health. It positively affects the resistance of the skin and the mucous membrane against chemical and physical irritation.

Vitamin C and bioflavonoids act synergistically to strengthen connective tissue in the blood vessel walls. This increases the resistance and integrity of the vessels and improves circulation. Vitamin C is an antioxidant that helps reduce the harmful effects of UVB rays on epithelial cells. It also helps in the work of the immune and endocrine systems.

Vitamin E is a strong antioxidant that helps slow down the aging of cells caused by the harmful effects of free radicals. It protects skin from inflammation caused by UV rays and maintains skin moisture. It regulates the abnormal proliferation of the skin's surface layers.

Sleep

Why is sleep important for a baby?

Sleep is necessary for babies to rest and recover from the previous day, just like adults. But babies also grow and learn more intensely, which additionally exhausts a small organism. Sleep is as necessary as food, love, and care. Plus, parents can have a good break while their angels are sleeping.

Right place

Like an adult, a baby likes to have a comfortable, clean, and warm place to sleep. Although it may initially seem that the baby can sleep wherever you place her, she will soon show what she likes and what she doesn't. It's possible that in the beginning, your newborn may show fear of in the bed that you have meant for her. Don't be surprised by this – newborns are tiny, and the crib is huge for them. Find her a little smaller place: an old cradle, a basket, a stroller, or a carrier.

Calming movements

While your baby was in the womb, you could notice how calm it was when you were moving, and that it started moving when you were still. When you want to calm your baby down, it's the same principle: take her in your arms and rock her lightly. These movements are perfect for lulling her to sleep.

Soothing sounds

While in your womb, the baby was entertained yet also calmed by different sounds: your heartbeat, stomach noises, voice. Obviously, you can't provide her with all these sounds now, but don't leave her in total silence. She is accustomed to background sounds, so provide them for her. The best toys for that purpose are those that repeat the same, calming music over and over again. Leave a TV on in another room or music or any home appliances that produce consistent sound (a fan, computer, blow dryer, or vacuum cleaner).

Baby's room

If the baby does not already have a separate room, the bedroom is completely fine. Silence and peace are needed for a healthy baby's sleep. However, don't be so far away from her that you can't hear her cry. The baby monitor can serve the purpose well – it's important to respond in time when the baby begins to cry and so avoid any hysterical screaming.

Daily naps

If the baby does not get enough sleep during the day, it can be nervous and resist sleep at night. A mistake that some parents make is to try to keep their babies awake during the day so that they'll sleep more at night. But in such cases, sleep will only be limited.

Good fresh air during the day also contributes to a good night's sleep, but be careful during the winter.

Why are rituals important to sleep?

The sooner a baby gets used to bedtime rituals, the better. As soon as the baby is born, you can start with some routines (such as bathing, dressing her in pajamas, nursing) and repeat them every evening at the same time, if possible. The baby will quickly and easily understand the consistency and predictability of the ritual, and will find it difficult to fall asleep without it.

Why does this work?

The baby feels calmer and more relaxed when she knows what's coming next. Perhaps you can fall asleep as soon as you lie down in your bed and turn off the light, but it's not possible for a baby. The baby will find it easier to fall asleep if she is completely relaxed and when it's quite clear what will follow (nursing, some quiet game, a lullaby). Keep the ritual going even when you are not at home, and also explain to the person who will care for her when you and your partner go out, the specific ritual your baby is used to.

Burning energy

Before bedtime, let the baby burn surplus energy. Let her jump and dance, tickle her to make her laugh. Let her differentiate between the kinds of game in the bathtub and the bed (such as reading a bedtime story) that should be warmer and calmer. Energy burning should be the first step to sleep.

Bathing

Teach your baby that bathing means the end of the day and, possibly, the last bedtime game. Babies like to bathe because it means enjoying the warm water, splashing, "swimming," laughing and playing with mom or dad, being naked. We remind you that bathing can be especially reserved for dad, especially if you are breastfeeding and he can't participates in feeding.

Little duties before sleep

Once the baby learns to sit, you can begin to put her on the potty, to introduce her to peeing and pooping outside the diaper. Another important thing that a child needs to adopt is tooth brushing. Experts advise that brushing can start as soon as the first tooth appears.

After bathing, it's time for caring rituals: applying lotion, taking vitamins prescribed by the pediatrician, dressing in pajamas, using a sleep sack, and so on.

Quiet games

Playing some quiet baby games on your bed is an excellent opportunity for spending a little more quality time with her. A quiet game involves fun for you and your baby, without making her too excited. For example, playing with her fingers by touching them one by one and singing the "Finger Family" song. Another fun idea is to hide something (a teddy bear, a cube, a toy) in her bed so that you look for it together before you put her to sleep. When an interesting item is found and you place it next to her, you can continue to play and talk.

Chatting

Bedtime is the right time for mom and dad to talk to their baby. You don't have to wait until your baby grows up to talk to her. There are many topics—if you can't think of anything, talk about what you and the baby did that day. Although the baby still does not understand you, your voice will relax her and calm her down, so she can fall asleep easily.

Wish the moon good night

Many babies love to be carried around the room or the home before they go to sleep, wishing everyone good night. When we say everyone, we mean it: all family members, favorite toys, furniture, even the moon.

Bedtime story

This is a classic bedtime ritual that you can begin as soon as the newborn arrives, despite the fact it doesn't understand the story. The baby will learn to recognize the tones and melodies of her mother tongue and quickly recognize new words when she hears them. Studies have shown that it is extremely important how many new words a baby hears every day. This can determine her speech skills and even intelligence.

Lullaby

Feel free to sing lullabies to your baby even if you are not talented. She is no music critic and will not mind if you don't really know how. Singing a lullabies is one of the oldest ways to lull a baby to sleep. Babies love to listen to the sound of their mother's voice, and the smooth and pleasant melody of the lullaby will soothe it. The repertoire is not crucial − it can be some of your favorite rock or pop melodies, and you can repeat the same song every night.

Let some nice music play

You don't have to sing; you can also turn on the radio or play calming music. It can be classical music, old folk lullabies, ambient music, children's songs, the choice is up to you. Calming music will help the baby to fall asleep and to elude any external noise.

How much should a baby sleep during the day, and how much during the night?

Parents often worry if their children sleep enough and how much is enough. There is a general guide to how much your baby should sleep every day. Of course, every child is different: some need a little more sleep and others need a little less.

In the first year and especially in the first months, a baby sleeps a lot during the day, so it may seem to sleep all day. As the child gets older, night sleep is prolonged.

Newborns up to a month
In the first weeks, your baby will probably sleep around fifteen to sixteen hours a day: about eight hours during the night (with occasional feeding and changing breaks) and about seven hours during the day (of course, not all seven hours at once, but a few times during the day).

Baby up to three months
Your baby still needs about fifteen hours of sleep, with night-time sleeping of about nine hours (with night-time feeding and changing), and daily naps are shortened a little.

Baby up to six months
A six-month-old baby needs about fourteen to fifteen hours of sleep a day. However, now night sleep takes up around eleven

hours, and daily naps about three to four hours. Also, now the baby is much livelier during the day.
Babies up to nine months

A nine-month-old baby needs about fourteen hours of sleep a day. Babies at this age sleep around eleven hours a night, and there is much less waking ups. Exceptions are the phases when the baby is teething or when she's cold or warm during the night, and if she experiences hunger.

Baby for up to twelve months
A one-year-old little one sleeps about two to three hours during the day (usually during the afternoon, or about an hour before noon and an hour afternoon) and around ten to eleven hours during the night.

Can I do something to help my baby sleep longer in the morning?

Most parents complain that their babies wake up too early in the morning. There are two types of little ones: those who are simply early birds and those who awaking without having rested enough.

To make sure your baby is sleeping enough, observe her reactions during the day. If she looks sleepy or falls asleep again for an hour or two after waking, something may be bothering her, so try to understand the reason (there might be too much light in the morning, or she has a full diaper, or someone in the family who wakes up early accidentally wakes up the baby, too).

If you feel that your little one gets up too early, try to move her bedtime progressively. If she goes to bed at about 7:00 to 8:00 in the evening, it's normal that she wakes up around 5:00 to 6:00 in the morning. However, keep in mind that the baby shouldn't go to sleep late—no later than 10:00 p.m.

How can I teach a child healthy sleep habits?

From the sixth month on, the baby should get used to a daily sleep ritual. This strategy should include:

Nightly ritual

Your child should go to bed at about the same time each evening. Practice the same rituals every night, even when you are not at home. Children love when their habits do not change; they prefer to know what will happen and when.

Daily schedule

Try to make a plan for the day, which includes when the baby sleeps, eats, plays, bathes, and goes to bed. When you adhere to some day-to-day rules, the child will eventually learn when it's time for which activity and when it's time to sleep, so it won't be nervous.

Teach your child to put herself to sleep

Try to teach your child to gradually sleep alone. This will not only be beneficial to you because you won't have to carry your baby constantly, but it will help your little one as well. If she wakes up in the night, she won't cry and will be able to calm herself.

A Baby-Friendly House

What small changes can I make to ensure my house safe for the baby?

- Put covers on the electrical sockets.

- Place protection on the drawers, bathroom, refrigerator, edges of tables, doors, stove regulators, the oven door, and other potentially dangerous objects.

- Place a protective fence on the staircase.

- Remove ashtrays from your child's sight. It would be best not to smoke at your home at all.

- Attach cabinets and shelves to the walls, so that the child can't pull them off.

- Hide electrical cords (place them under a protective covering, stuck to the floor with a special tape or hidden behind furniture).

- Place the house plants out of the child's reach.

- Check all screws on the furniture and tighten them.

- Place protective grids in front of the fireplace, stove, heater, radiator.

- Forget about using tablecloths for a while—the baby can pull them off and cause huge accidents with the dishes, etc.

- Babies should not play with older children's toys. They are not suitable for their age and they can be injured.

- Put all chemicals out of reach of the child.

- Keep all medicines out of reach of the child (including toothpaste, vitamins, hair shampoo).

- Do not leave any of the following in the child's reach: coins, marbles, things with less than two inches (3.5 cm) in diameter, scissors, knives, razors, matches, lighters, pens, plastic bags or balloons, jewelry, and so on.

Playing with Your Baby

How can I play with my baby at three months?

Many games will not have any effect unless you repeat them frequently. Baby's attention span varies for a lot of reasons. It's not just because of the age; sometimes it's temperament, but also her mood. She will sometimes enjoy playing, but more often than not, you will have to adapt the game to her instincts.

Whatever happens, don't get upset or panic. The important thing is that you are playing and doing your best. That way, you are encouraging the baby's development and also building a better emotional connection.

Note: Each of these games is safe and does not cost anything. It will help you spend a lot of quality time together, which is precious for both the baby and you. All you need to do is repeat the same games more often and to improve them, depending on your child's wishes.

Dance Revolution

When a baby has colic, nothing is better than good music and a little dancing. Let some relaxing music play, combine genres, and see what your baby likes. Hold her close and dance with her. In the beginning, gently swing, sing, and then later, depending on the baby's age, include new dance moves.

If she gets upset when you pick her up, dress as colorful as you can and dance. Your performance will entertain her.

Let's Find Things

Most of your time in raising a child will be dedicated to showing her things, educating her. This starts with newborns. New babies adore a variety of colors, textures, fragrances, and tastes. Babies use all of the senses to introduce new objects, and they have to try everything.

You don't have to buy many baby storybooks. It's enough to have one or two and read them to your child. Of course, always include the baby as you read. It's clear that the baby will not understand a word of what you are reading to her, but will eventually understand that this book means socializing with you, and will begin to enjoy this time.

In addition to books, use everything you have. Make her rattles of various shapes and sizes from old bottles, and familiarize the baby with the objects that surround her.

Touch Me

Your baby explores the world with all of her senses. Let her touch you, smell you, feel your closeness. Give her a chance to explore different textures. Offer her silk, cashmere, or cotton to touch. Tickle her hands and toes with some gentle cloth or a feather. She will enjoy hanging out with you.

Peek-a-Boo

This is a great game that includes all the senses. With a soft cloth (preferably cotton), you can easily cover your baby's face, and then put it aside for the baby to see you. Repeat this a few times, and your baby will be a happy baby.

Are games for four-month-olds more physically demanding?

At this age, the baby will become more physically active. She starts to turn, and she may even try to sit up. During this period, she can hold objects in her hands, but also her mouth, and spend most of the day doing similar things.

Games can now become more physically demanding. The baby probably enjoys games that require tickling. She tries to answer you and keeps track of you wherever you go.

Smell Different Scents

Are you in the kitchen? Are you trying to make something for dinner and the baby does not stop looking at you? You can make this fun for the baby as well. Take various spices and slowly bring them closer to her; let her experience various scents. Get her acquainted with vanilla, cinnamon, pepper, and flour (be careful that spices are not inhaled through the nose). The little one will enjoy discovering new aromas, and you will laugh because she will make funny expressions.

This game is a good one because you are getting know the baby and her character, discovering the smells she likes. You can try later to provide these scents in food and use air fresheners that the baby loves.

Bubbles, Bubbles All Around Me

There is something magical in soap bubbles, and your baby is now able to see clearly enough to focus on them from a certain distance.

Entertain the baby by blowing bubbles when she is restless, while you are waiting for a bus, or you want to dry her tears. Blow bubbles even in the park to invite others, children a little older, to entertain and keep your baby company.

Bubbles are cheap fun, easy to carry, easy to make, and your baby will be infinitely fascinated by them.

I'll Catch You

At this age, babies are old enough to understand different connotations of voice and language. No baby can resist when you say this and you're tickling, hugging, tossing her in the air, and covering her in kisses.

You can approach your baby with similar words: "What are you up to? Wait till I get you (tickling), and toss you high (tossing her in the air), and hug you and kiss you (hugging and kissing)." This, like all other games, should be repeated several times.

A Little Pig

This game is a famous one. Although not pleasant for older children, babies from four to six months are more than entertained. They do not understand a word, but it's important to talk to them while you're tickling their toes.

"This little piglet went to market. This little piglet stayed home. This little piggy had roast beef. This little piglet had none. And this piglet cried, 'Wee wee wee, I want some'" (squeeze and tickle the toes from the pinky to the big toe).

It's Time for Dinner

Most of you have already experienced this type of game. Ticklish people generally don't like it, but babies enjoy it because they are surrounded by the people they love.

Raise your baby's shirt, put your lips to her stomach, and blow a raspberry. It sounds like a whoopee cushion or farting. Babies enjoy this hugely.

Flying, Baby, Flying

When a baby can hold her head up on her own, it's a sign that you can toss her in various directions, not only up. Help her fly outside and grab leaves. If you are in the house, help her touch the ceiling or the top of the closet. Help your baby discover the world from different perspectives. You also like to see things from a different angle, right?

How can I play with a baby from seven to nine months?

The baby in this period becomes a real expert in sitting and will soon be able to crawl. Encourage the child's every step by applauding and supporting each new change: "Good job sitting down!"

During this period, they also manage to capture objects and switch them from hand to hand. They successfully control their hand movements.

They also begin to understand object permanence and know that an object you hide does not disappear from the face of the earth, but is somewhere nearby.

Touch, Grab, and Throw

If your baby is holding an object in her hand, she is likely to throw it on the floor. If the objects are held in both hands, it's likely that they will be thrown to the floor. And so on, indefinitely – first with one hand, then the other.

Babies will look at these objects intently, study them, taste them a little, and throw them to the floor to hear how they sound.

At this stage, your baby begins to understand the sound, and so it's important that you don't forbid her throwing things (of course, they must be objects that can't hurt her or others).

Support the baby in this activity. Pick up the thrown objects and give them to her again if she can't get them on her own. Let your baby be a little scientist.

I Can Handle Things!

At this age, it's important to teach your child to turn lights on and off, use the doorbell, and the remote control. Imagine her excitement when she discovers that pressing a button makes completely different things happen. This delights kids.

Support your child in this kind of play. Let her try to control things with her own hands. Let her explore what really happens when she presses buttons.

Let's Move Objects!

If a baby can already crawl or walk, it's very likely that she will move things from one place to another. It's a great game for the development of motor skills.

Don't prevent her from lifting and carrying pillows and other things. If she wasn't able, she wouldn't do it. Allow her to "struggle" with things and discover how to easily transfer objects from one place to another.

Hiding Games a Hundred Ways

Play hide and seek in all possible ways. Hide yourself, hide objects, let the baby hide. You have numerous options. The baby gains confidence with these games, knowing that her parents are always with her, even when she cannot see them. If the baby just covers her head, you do not have to find her right away – pretend you can't see her.

Rolling a Ball

Babies adore balls. They adore when you throw a ball in the air and it falls back to the floor, or when they drop a ball and it falls to the floor. They adore it when balls roll.

In the beginning, they will laugh and try to catch the ball, but eventually, they'll start to throw you the ball or kick it. In a couple of years, you'll be able to play a match together.

How can you play with a baby from the tenth to the twelfth month?

Your baby is not a baby anymore, she's nearly a child. Most popular games at this stage are those that help develop motor skills. Babies are already confident in moving on their feet; they know the environment and the direction they're going.

Babies at this age can strengthen their hands by squeezing objects and crumpling papers. It's a good idea to give them a notebook only for them, and to keep important papers and documents in a high place.

Assembling and Dismantling

During this period, it's natural for babies to grasp the connection between the objects, so they can start classifying their similarities: putting all rounded objects in round places, squares with cubed objects, and the like.

There are great games for classifying colors, shapes, and dimensions. You do not need to buy expensive building blocks, just find items in the house that are safe for playing, and give them tasks. You can sit and supervise while they play with pleasure.

If kids ask for help, you should help them. But after a few repeated actions, encourage them to try for themselves.

Repeat This, Baby

In addition to motor skills, babies also develop the ability to imitate how you yawn, how you laugh, how you say, "Oh." It's all fascinating to them. Encourage her to imitate you.

Swimming = Fun

Older babies can take care of themselves in the tub. Of course, only use a little water that can't cover them when they lie down, plenty of soap, and they will enjoy their bath.

Sit next to the baby while she is bathing, splash her, make foam and shapes out of foam, rub her hair, make a foam mustache. Whatever comes to mind − children love bath time.

Give her toys and don't worry. She'll enjoy playing in the water for a while. From time to time, add some warm water so that she isn't sitting in cold water.

After bathing, play with a towel together, dry the toys, dry the baby. And with a little luck, the child is clean, smiling and ready to sleep. Isn't that fun?

What Babies Like

1. Mommy's face

The baby first recognizes your head shape and hairstyle. When your newborn does not sleep, she usually spends her time looking at you. Since babies see only eight to twelve inches (20 to 30 cm) away, this is the perfect distance between your face and your little one when you nurse. When it's two months old, the baby recognizes your face and reacts to your appearance with a smile. It is interesting that the baby initially recognizes your head shape, hairstyle, and chin, and only later recognizes your eyes, nose, and mouth.

Although you might think your newborn does not understand, talk to her as much as possible, and with appropriate gestures. Ask her questions and answer them, make funny faces, lift your eyebrows and watch your baby react. Most will first look at it, and then try to imitate the movements.

2. Vibrant colors

Parents often choose pastel colors for the wardrobe, toys, and bedding. However, research has shown that babies love and enjoy bright colors, especially red, purple, and blue.

This applies to babies three to four months old because they have not seen colors before, only the faint outlines.

3. Music

Little ones simply adore the sound of bells and musical toys (especially those turning in mobiles over the crib). Interestingly, at the earliest age, babies can show affection for certain types of music, while other kinds disturb them. Also, babies demonstrate very early on whether they have a sense of rhythm, so some move completely to the rhythm of music, while others don't.

What all the babies like is to create their own music. For the beginning, it is a rattle, and later the first musical instruments.

4. Older children

The main reason why babies like older children (about three years old) is that they still have a high voice that is very pleasurable to them. Also, they like other children's movements and emotions, but also the fact that they are still little and more similar to them.

5. Touch (cuddling, tickling)

Babies enjoy touch, especially in massage and tickling, because they get extra attention this way. Babies find the massage delightful, while tickling entertains them. Between the fourth and sixth months, they react with giggling and laughter.

6. Remote control

A child usually shows interest in the remote control from the sixteenth month on when she tries to imitate your actions. It's fun to press buttons of various shapes and colors, and to observe what happens next.

Children are also fascinated by mobile phones that light up and ring, and respond when pressed. Even more challenging for them is the fact that they are off-limits.

7. Animals

Animals have an incredible effect on babies. If you have a pet, the child feels you love her, so she feels safe. Also, most parents are delighted to show their children dogs or cats in public. Babies feel that the living being is more exciting than a toy because its movements are unpredictable, entertaining, and they simply enjoy watching and playing with animals.

8. Hiding games

A game of hiding or peek-a-boo is one of the funniest for babies. Before the eighth month, a baby thinks that everything hidden has disappeared for good. However, at nine to ten months, children know that you are here, eagerly waiting to appear or look for you. By the time the baby initiates this game, she puts her hands over her eyes or hides behind objects with the intention of surprising you.

9. Luminous jewelry

Shimmering things attract children's attention – earrings that dangle, but also necklaces. Jewelry sparkles in the light, and the baby cannot take her eyes off of it, even in trying to get it. Such reactions are possible from the fourth month, so be careful as this is the period when the baby examines objects by putting them in her mouth.

Conclusion

No one said that parenting was going to be easy (if they did, they lied). Being a parent is a full-time job with no weekends or vacations, and it lasts for the rest of your life. Yet although it may sound scary, it's also the most pleasurable and rewarding job on the planet. That little human being is coming to make you a different, better person than you could ever imagine yourself to be.

There will be ups and downs, wonderful and difficult times. But with a lot of love, and a reliable book with solutions to your dilemmas, you're at the great beginning of a marvelous journey.

Printed in Great Britain
by Amazon